The

Woman's

Book of

Questions

The *Woman's* Book of Questions

Sophia Mark

MJF BOOKS
NEW YORK

Published by MJF Books
Fine Communications
322 Eighth Avenue
New York, NY 10001

The Woman's Book of Questions
ISBN 1-56731-694-8
Library of Congress Number 2004106410

Manufactured in the United States of America on
acid-free paper ∞

MJF Books and the MJF colophon are trademarks of
Fine Creative Media, Inc.

MV   12   11   10   9   8   7   6   5   4   3   2   1

THE WOMAN'S BOOK OF QUESTIONS

✤

201 Bold, Sinfully Provocative Questions to Ask
Yourself and Your Friends

by Sophia Mark

What would you do if you came home
unexpectedly and found your man dressed in
your lace bra and panties?

Welcome to *The Woman's Book of Questions*—a collection of outrageous and sinfully provocative questions for women to ask themselves and their best friends. Women have always learned from one another, sharing personal stories, wisdom, experience, joys, and anxieties. We love exploring ideas with someone else, putting ourselves in our friends' shoes (or clothes, for that matter), expressing our own values through the advice we give others.

So when we got together—a group of women of assorted age, ethnic, and socioeconomic groups—to have a little fun, it occurred to us that the intimate stories we were bandying about could give rise to a whole batch of candid and stimulating questions. Once we started writing down those questions, they prompted more spicy stories and more questions, until we felt the need to share our experience in this book.

The Woman's Book of Questions supplies food for thought—a whole feast, in fact—on subjects close to a woman's heart. Here you will find stimulating, difficult, and, yes, sometimes *embarrassing* questions to ask yourself—and your friends—about sex, love, motherhood, friendship, family, beauty, body image, shopping, fears, feelings, and fantasies.

The Woman's Book of Questions is as much fun as a night out with the girls, as revealing as years of therapy, and as informative as a college seminar. As every philosopher, journalist, detective, teacher, psychologist, and mother knows, asking the right questions is the quickest route to valuable information, revelation, and self-discovery. Now you have permission to consider out loud those brash, delicious questions that can be both unnerving and energizing.

In this book you'll find a whole range of engaging questions. Some will immediately reconnect you to personal experiences from your past; others will require a leap of imagination into a hypothetical situation. Some will draw on the wisdom you've acquired from observing the lives of other women, and still others will encourage you to look inside and examine your most deeply held values. Some questions can be considered while you're waiting for a bus; others will linger with you throughout the day.

To encourage browsing, *The Woman's Book of Questions* is arranged in no particular order. Open it to any page—at home, in the office, on the train, in the bathroom, in bed. To explore it best, share it with friends at a party, over lunch, at a soccer game, at the coffee machine, or at the hairdresser's. Every page has a question that will start you thinking, remembering, and connecting with your experiences and with other women. Best of all, there are no right answers! *The Woman's Book of Questions* is a catalyst for conversation among friends—or the starting point of a dialogue with yourself.

The

Woman's

Book of

Questions

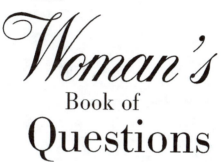

1

Would you tell your friend if you knew her husband was cheating? Would you tell her husband if she were the cheater? What if the situation were reversed: would you want to be told?

2

If you committed indiscretions in your youth,
such as taking drugs or having many sexual
partners, would you tell your children?
For what reasons?

3

Have you ever secretly gone through your boyfriend's or husband's pockets or dresser drawers? Your child's? If so, why?

4

Do you believe in woman's intuition?

5

Have you ever felt you would give your life
for someone else? For a cause?

6

Which is worse—not shaving your armpits for three months or not combing your hair for three months?

7

Your doctor has told you that you can never have children. How do you reveal this to your fiancé or husband?

To what extent would you be willing to lie or forge documents to get your child into a good school? For example, would you falsify your address or ask a friend who lives in that district to let you use her address?

9

What three areas of compatibility are most important to you when considering an intimate relationship with someone—sexual attraction, personal hygiene, profession, religion, etc.?

10

If your beloved partner died first, could you
ever seek another? What would your
partner do if you died first?

11

If a stranger offered you $100,000 for one night of sex, and you knew that it was safe, payment was guaranteed, and no one would ever find out, would you do it?

12

What has been the biggest disappointment
in your life? The biggest surprise?
The greatest joy?

13

Have you ever thought of abandoning your husband and children and starting life over somewhere else?

14

If you had four days in which to do anything you wanted but had to do it alone, what would you do? Would you be content being on your own?

15

Do you like to cook? How did you learn? What is your most successful dish? Your biggest failure?

16

Approximately how many times a day do you look in the mirror? If you were to avoid your reflection for a whole day, how would you feel?

17

Would you get rid of your period forever if you wouldn't lose your ability to conceive?

18

Would it make any difference in your
feelings for your grandchildren if they were
racially mixed? If they were
brought up in a different religion?

19

Do you regret the number of sexual partners
you have had? Do you wish you'd had more?
Fewer? Why?

20

Have you ever considered plastic surgery to increase or reduce the size of your breasts? If so, what effect do you think the surgery would have on you? On others?

21

When you regret things in your life, is it for things you have done that you wish you hadn't, or for things you have *not* done that you wish you *had*?

22

What would you do if you came home unexpectedly and found your man dressed in your lace bra and panties?

23

Do you think it's true that black men are sexually well endowed? What about other stereotypes, such as "Jews are good at business" or "Women nag"— are they truth or myth?

24

Would you have an affair with your
best friend's husband if you felt he
was your soulmate?

25

If your teenage child announced he or
she were gay, what would you say?
How would you feel?

26

Would you be willing to donate an egg to
your friend if she and her partner were
unable to conceive? Would you be willing
to become a surrogate mother and
carry the baby for them?

27

Have you ever pretended to be interested in a sport in order to impress a date? Have you ever deliberately lost a game or played poorly so as not to show up your date?

28

What would you do if you and your friend went shopping together and both wanted to buy the same dress—but there was only one?

29

What was your favorite toy when you were a child? Why did you love it? Which is the toy you wanted most but never had?

30

What would be the most enjoyable way to
spend an evening with your partner?
Would your partner agree?

31

What is the nastiest thing you've ever done?
Do you regret it?

32

If you're a mother and you had it to do over again, would you have had any children? More children? Fewer?

33

When you are sad or upset, what activity do you usually pursue to comfort yourself? Eating? Cleaning? Drinking? Working? Shopping? Exercise? Sex? Something else?

34

What makes you jealous? Do you suffer
jealous feelings silently or show
them in some way?

35

Have you ever taken out an ad in a personals
column? Ever answered one?
What happened?

36

What is your first memory of your mother, your father, or the people who raised you?

37

Have you ever gone through your mother's
closet? What were you looking for?
What did you find?

38

Have you ever been attracted to another
woman—emotionally, physically, or sexually?
Would you consider having a female partner?
Or, if you've primarily been with women,
would you consider having a male partner?

~:❀:~

39

Have you ever wished you were a man?

40

If you could turn back the hands of time
to relive one special event in your life,
what would it be?

41

What is the biggest risk you've ever taken?
Was it worth it?

❀

42

Do you have a secret bank account? Ever
wish you had one?

43

If you were caught in a fire or a flood and could save only one person—your husband or your child—which would you choose?

44

Have you ever tried to talk your way out of a traffic ticket by flirting with the policeman, pretending you were too ignorant to understand what you had done wrong, or bursting into tears?

45

Would you consider adopting a child? Would
you adopt a baby of a different race or
nationality? An older child? A child with
a disability or a troubled past?

46

Have you ever dyed your hair? Had plastic
surgery? How far would you go to change
your appearance?

47

Have you ever been completely or partially naked in public? At a nude beach? At a nudist camp or colony? In your backyard? Did you like it?

48

Do you have any clothes in your closet that you have kept over the years for sentimental reasons? What do they mean to you?

49

Have you ever been in a physical fight with another woman? With a man? What happened to bring you to that point?

50

Do you find that you relate better to men
than to women, or vice versa?

51

Is there some common activity (cooking, driving, swimming, socializing, or something else) that secretly scares you?

52

What would you do if you learned your husband had been married before and had not told you? What if he had children he hadn't mentioned?

53

If you knew your teenager had committed a minor crime, would you lie—even under oath—to protect him or her from the authorities? What if the crime were serious?

54

If the man you loved did not want children but you were desperate to have one, would you consider an "accidental" pregnancy?

55

Have you ever done something you were
really ashamed of? Have you ever
revealed it to a friend?

❖

56

What is the longest you've gone without a
shower? How did you feel about your body
odor? Do you think male body odor is sexy?

57

Have you ever used flirtation, sex, or the
promise of sex to get ahead in your career?
Do you automatically suspect an
attractive, successful woman of having
granted sexual favors?

58

Do you believe your dreams are significant?
How?

❀

59

Have you ever said or done something to
your child that you will always regret? Has
one of your parents ever said or done
something to you that you will never
forget—or forgive?

60

Have you ever lied about your cultural or religious background in order to "blend in"?

61

Suppose you were pregnant and learned that your child would have a severe physical deformity or be mentally handicapped. Would you have the baby?

62

Would you rather have a series of exciting, passionate love affairs or a sustaining, long-term relationship?

63

If your lover asked you to do something you felt was kinky, would you do it? Why? To see if you like it, or just to please?

64

What was the last nice thing you did for someone you know? For a stranger? What was the last nice thing someone did for you?

65

If your daughter tells you she wants to grow up to be president of the United States and asks why there have been no female presidents, what do you tell her?

66

Are there female principles and qualities that are more conducive to negotiations for peace than male qualities? What are they? How do they show up in your personal life?

67

What qualities seem to you to be distinctly female or distinctly male? What qualities seem to unite the sexes? Divide the sexes?

68

Would you tell a friend if her favorite outfit looked horrible on her?

69

Do you have a secret stash of something (for example, candy, alcohol, money) hidden somewhere in the house?

70

Have you ever called in sick in order
to go shopping?

71

If you knew that your father was cheating on your mother, would you tell her? What if your mother was the one doing the cheating?

72

How many handbags do you have? How many pairs of shoes? Do you have too few, too many, or just about the right number?

73

Have you ever let a man buy you a drink even though he didn't have a chance with you?

74

How many diets have you tried? If they haven't worked, why not? Will you try again?

75

Does it bother you to be in messy surroundings? How important is it to you to live in a clean, well-run household?

76

Do you buy presents for your pet? Do you think this makes your pet love you more?

✿

77

What was the weirdest or funniest blind date you ever had?

78

When do you choose to sleep naked?

79

Is the way to a man's heart really
through his stomach?

80

Do you ever go without underwear?
Under what circumstances?
Have you ever been discovered?

81

What's the most humiliating thing that has ever happened to you?

✤

82

Which three words best describe the three things you find most frustrating about yourself?

83

If you had to choose one, would you rather be most successful in dance, drama, education, architecture, science, literature, finance, or parenting? If you could choose another area of expertise, what would it be?

84

How often do you think you know what someone is thinking? Do you ever act on such an assumption?

❧❀❧

85

Have you ever contacted an old boyfriend you haven't seen or heard from in years? If so, why?

86

Have you ever questioned or thought of giving up the religion in which you were brought up?

87

Do you believe that wearing a burka (a head-to-toe covering) liberates women from being treated according to their beauty or their feminine attributes? What would you say to a woman who feels that this is true?

88

Have you ever made love to someone you had met only hours before? Have you ever made love to someone without exchanging names? Was it exciting? Why?

89

If you could live one day as another type of person (a different gender, culture, faith, family unit, or set of personal attributes), which would you choose?

90

If you won $1,000,000, would you give
some of it to charity? How much?
Which organization? What would you do
with the rest of it?

91

Would you marry someone to help him get a green card? Would you marry someone you didn't love in order to get a green card?

~·✾·~

92

Do women make better bosses than men? Which gender would you rather report to?

93

What tradition did your family celebrate
when you were a child that you still
celebrate today?

94

Can a man and a woman really have a
sustained platonic relationship and
not cross the line into sex?

95

How would you feel if you discovered that
your good friend was gay or bisexual?
What would you do?

96

If you were to witness an act of verbal "race baiting" or discrimination, would you turn your head and act as if you didn't see it? What if the encounter became physical? What would you do if someone in your social circle made a joke that was clearly a racial slur?

97

Would you ever cheat on an important exam?
If not, what would you do if a good
friend did so?

98

Have you ever lied on your resume to help get a position you were after?

99

Have you ever stolen something even though you had the money to pay for it?

100

Would you be upset if your child wanted to marry someone from a different race or religion? Someone poor? Uneducated? Disabled? Someone of the same sex? Which would you find the most difficult to accept?

101

How would you feel if your adult children asked you to babysit for their kids while they took a week's vacation in the south of France?

102

Do you remember your first menstrual cycle?
Where were you? What did you feel?

103

What is the most memorable or meaningful gift you've ever received from one of your children? From your partner? From a friend?

104

Who is your favorite fictional female character from a book or movie? What qualities does she have that you like so well?

105

How important is it for you to be married and have a family? Is there something wrong with women who never marry?

106

How important is it for you to have a life
beyond the one you have with your mate?
Do you encourage your mate to have
friendships that don't include you?

107

Are there many things you do or hope to do as you interact with your children that are different from what your own mother did?

108

What real-life woman do you most admire, and why? In politics? In the media? What woman, other than a friend or relative, has most influenced your life?

109

Is there a secret about yourself that you have never shared with anyone?

110

Have you ever faked an orgasm?

111

Would you marry a man you didn't love
for his money?

112

Do you think it is better to live with someone you don't love than to be alone?

113

If you had given up a child for adoption when you were young, would you tell your present partner?

114

If you could "freeze" yourself at a certain age or point in time, what age would you choose? Why?

115

Have you ever served a store-bought dish
to guests and taken credit for
making it yourself?

116

If you could change one thing in your life,
what would it be?

117

Do you ever feel that your daughter prefers
her mother-in-law to you?

118

What name have you asked or would you ask
your grandchildren to call you? Was this what
you called your grandmother?

119

Have you ever lied about the price of
something you bought?

120

If you saw a woman being attacked by a man on a dark, lonely street, what would you do?

121

You meet the man of your dreams but learn he has only a year to live. Do you pursue the relationship, or walk away to avoid feeling the pain of his inevitable death?

122

Do you have a lucky charm or an article of clothing you either wear or carry with you in situations that make you anxious? Where did you get it? Why does it make you feel better?

123

You have an elderly parent who can no longer live alone. You have room in your home, and money is not a consideration. Would you move your parent into your home? Into a nursing home? Hire someone to take care of your parent in his or her own home?

124

Your daughter has been offered a full scholarship to a B-list college. She has also been accepted at an Ivy League school, but with only a small stipend. Sending her to the Ivy League school is possible, but only with great sacrifice by the rest of the family. Which would you choose? Would your choice be different if the child were your son?

125

Have you ever lied about your age? Did you say you were older or younger?

126

You are single and in your late thirties to early forties, and your biological clock is ticking loudly. Would you marry a man you didn't love in order to have a child before it is too late, or would you become a single mother?

127

If you discovered you were adopted, would you search for your biological parents? What would you do if a child you had put up for adoption contacted you?

128

What is your significant other's most annoying habit? What is yours?

❀

129

If your child were starring in a school play on the day you had to give an important presentation at work, would you attend the play or give the presentation?

130

Which is more important to you: that your children are bright or well-liked? Why?

131

If you could wear only one outfit for a whole year, what would it be?

132

If you could have a steamy, illicit one-time affair and your significant other would never find out, would you do it? Would you want to know if your significant other had had a one-night stand?

133

Would you marry a man who was ten years younger than you? Would such an age difference become a problem?

134

Over the years, you have remembered the birthdays, sent the greeting cards, cooked the holiday dinners, and in general made all the arrangements for the family's social life. Now you are tired of carrying the burden alone. How do you get your husband to share in these tasks?

135

Have you ever wanted to be famous? How would fame affect your life?

~:❁:~

136

You and a man who is a stranger are shipwrecked on an island. What qualities do you each need to survive? How would things be different if the stranger were a woman?

137

How can you protect your children from
sexual abuse?

138

You have been lucky enough to acquire some wealth. How will you protect it for your children? How do you foresee them handling their inheritance after you die? At what age would you let them do as they pleased with it?

139

You have a daughter and a son, and each has children. How do you decide who will inherit your diamond engagement ring?

~:❀:~

140

Would you ever vacation without your partner? Why? Why not?

141

You usually have a drink in a local bar/restaurant with your partner, who is now out of town. Would you go to the same place and have a drink alone? How would you feel?

142

Have you ever padded your bra?
If so, were you found out?

❦

143

Which male and female physical types
attract you most?

144

Have you ever bought an expensive
dress for a special occasion and
returned it the next day?

145

Have you ever left a note for a
cute waiter or bartender?

146

Have you ever made a pass at a friend's
boyfriend? At your sister's boyfriend?

147

If you had a severely handicapped child who required so much of your emotional and financial resources that your other children felt neglected, would you put the child in an institution?

148

Does it bother you to go out with a man who is shorter than you are or makes less money than you do?

149

Have you ever hung up on a good friend? What caused you to do it? How long did you wait before you called back?

150

Have you ever broken off a long-term friendship with another woman because you couldn't forgive her for something she had done?

151

Do you spend a lot of money on sexy underwear? Why?

152

What would you do if your significant other gave you an expensive present that you hated? What if you were given no gift at all for a birthday or anniversary?

153

Under what circumstances have you lied to your parents about who you were going out with or where you were going? What would you do if you found out that your own child was lying to you?

154

Have you ever made up a story just to make
your lover or husband jealous?
What happened?

155

If you had twin daughters, would you dress them alike?

156

In what way, if at all, do you think changing the color of your hair would change the way people—especially men—treat you?

157

Have you ever pretended to be someone else in an electronic chat room?

158

Has being a woman restricted your
choices in life?

159

Should a couple stay together when they don't love each other—"for the sake of the children"?

160

What stops you from achieving a
feeling of contentment?

161

What single event in your past has had the
most detrimental effect on your life?

162

If you had only five minutes to live, what would you do? What if you had five days? Five weeks?

163

When you are angry at people, are you more likely to yell at them, give them the silent treatment, or just burst into tears?

164

You're alone and driving along a country road. A dog runs out in front of your car, and you swerve but can't help hitting it. What do you do next?

165

You are driving the family car and accidentally back up into a parked car. You have made a small dent in your own fender as well as in that of the parked car. No one has seen the accident. Do you leave a note for the owner of the other car or just drive away? Do you tell your husband?

166

Have you ever bitten your toenails?

∼:❀:∼

167

When you are upset, are you more likely to talk things over with a friend or your partner or to keep it to yourself?

168

Does saying something out loud—"I'm in love," "I'm going to move to another state," "I'm going to have a baby"—make it seem more real?

169

If you had to move to a different country,
which would it be?

170

How much would you give up for your partner? Your country? Your religion? Your job? Your family? Your children?

171

Do you favor one of your children
over the others? Why?

172

What is your favorite food? Your favorite dessert? Is there any food that you find absolutely irresistible? Has this preference changed since you were a child?

173

Would you adopt a child even if you could—
or did—have children of your own?

174

Do you think there should be forced sterilization for certain crimes such as rape and child molestation? If not for one instance, what about for repeat offenders?

175

Which would you rather have: a successful career helping people—as, say, a doctor, a lawyer, or a social worker—but without having children, or the opportunity to raise children and possibly sacrifice having such a career?

176

If you were told you had the gene for breast cancer, would you consider having a double mastectomy to guard against the disease?

177

Do you feel that children of mixed-race
parentage face disadvantages in
today's society?

178

You've taken your marriage vows seriously up to this point, but you are approached by a gorgeous man—and on more than one occasion. Do you admire him from afar, flirt innocently, or slip him your phone number?

179

At what age, if any, would you consider yourself a "spinster"? Can a single woman have as fulfilling a life as a married one? Are spinsters regarded as second-class citizens?

180

What would you do if your teenage daughter told you her boyfriend had been physically abusive toward her?

181

If you were sexually harassed by someone in your office, would you report the incident? Would you worry that in the end you would be the one with the most to lose?

182

Would you terminate a pregnancy that was the result of rape?

183

If you could live in any historical era, which one would you choose?

184

As a woman, which do you feel exists and affects you most in your work environment and everyday dealings: racism, sexism, elitism, or ageism?

185

Have you ever deliberately ignored your daughter's (or daughter-in-law's) directive against feeding your grandchildren "junk food"?

186

Have you ever felt that your children love their father more than you, even though you have done the most for and with them?

187

If, with one wish, you could cause a person
to disappear, who would it be?

188

Do you remember what you wore on important occasions in your life?

∴❀∵

189

What are you most proud of?

190

Do you have any women friends who are
significantly older or younger than you?
What is it about them that you like?
Why do you think they like you?

191

Do you have any close friends of a different race? If not, why not? Would you like to?

192

When you had intercourse for the first time, were you disappointed? Surprised? Relieved? Awestruck? Scared?

193

Do you talk to yourself when you are alone?
Why?

❀

194

When you look toward your future, what
scares you most?

195

Your eightieth birthday is approaching. You are in poor health, and the doctor advises you not to travel. But you live on the West Coast; your two older sisters live in the East; and you long to celebrate this birthday with them. Do you ignore the doctor's orders?

196

Your mother always criticized you when you were growing up. Now she criticizes the way you are bringing up your kids. What do you do?

197

Do you ever tell lies to make people believe you are more popular or successful than you feel you are? Why?

198

You have become intimate with a man who tries to make love to you but can't sustain an erection. How do you feel? What do you do?

199

At your neighbors' moving sale you notice a painting you are sure is a Picasso. You know these neighbors really need money. Do you tell them the truth about the painting or buy it yourself for the $5 asking price?

200

You see a woman slapping and yelling at her small child in the street. Do you intervene?

201

Is life worth questioning, or is it better to just live it?